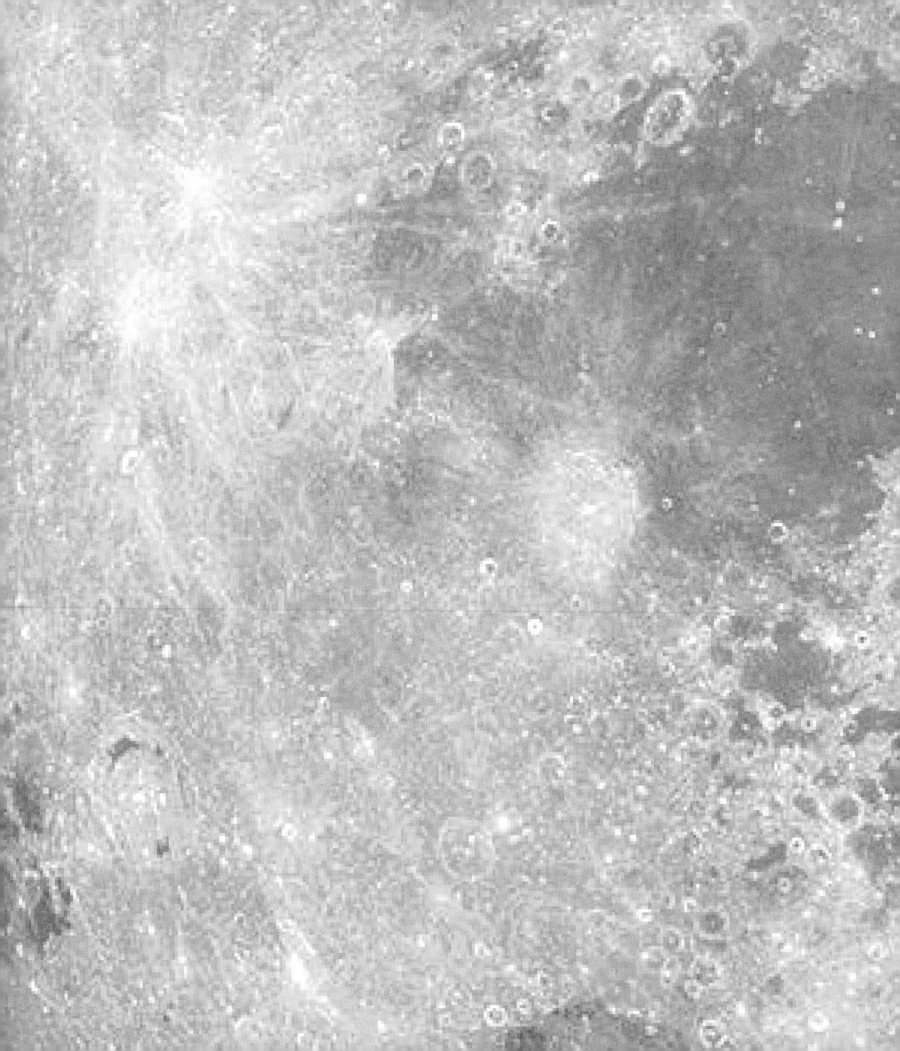

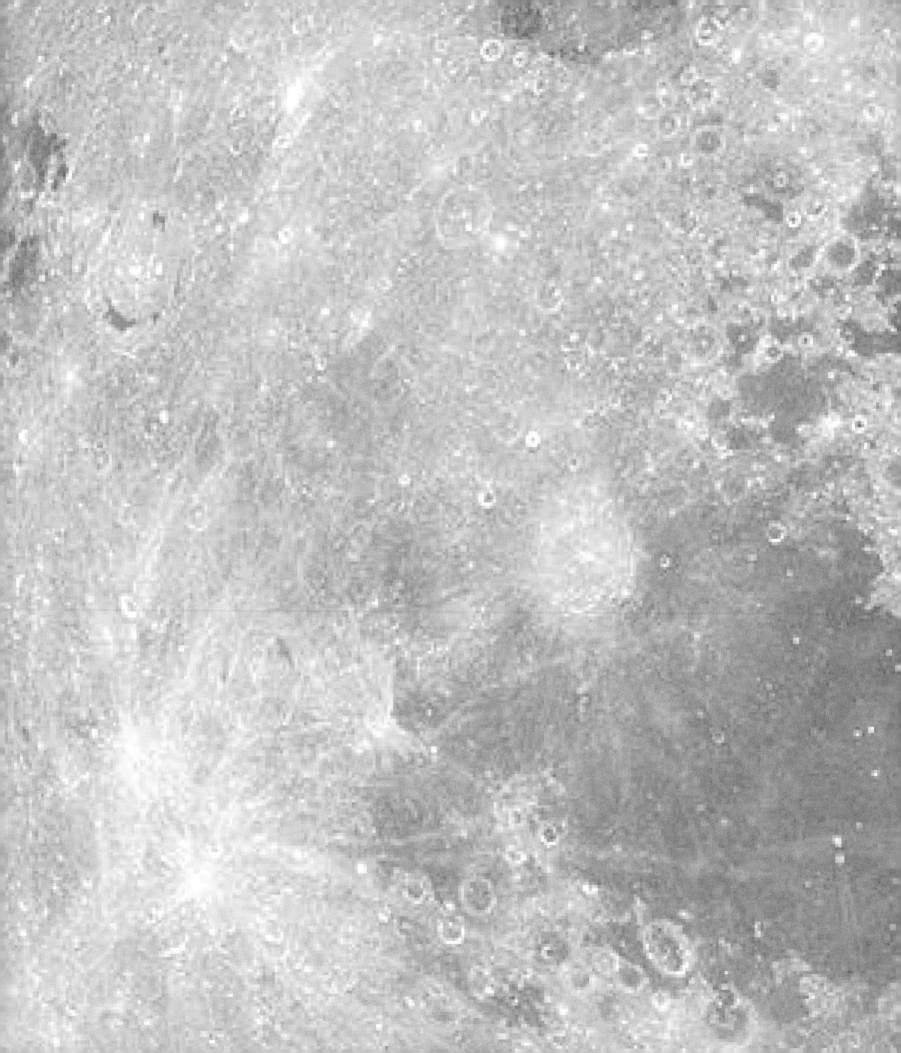

Countdown

2979 Days to the Moon

With love to the adventurous Buckingham brothers, George and Fred.
—S. S.

To all the astronauts who spearheaded this crazy, monumental
idea that humans could travel beyond our own world.
And to my wife Noni and daughter Nina, who had to listen to me
about the exploits of the astronauts and how impressed I was with their
character and determination, over and over…and over.
—T. G.

Ω

Published by
PEACHTREE PUBLISHERS
1700 Chattahoochee Avenue
Atlanta, Georgia 30318-2112
www.peachtree-online.com

Text © 2018 by Suzanne Slade
Illustrations © 2018 by Thomas Gonzalez

Edited by Kathy Landwehr
Design and composition by Nicola Simmonds Carmack
Copy edited by Vicky Holifield

The illustrations were rendered in pastel, colored pencil, and airbrush.

Printed in February 2018 by R.R. Donnelley in China
10 9 8 7 6 5 4 3 2 1
First Edition
978-1-68263-013-6

Library of Congress Cataloging-in-Publication Data

Names: Slade, Suzanne, author. | Gonzalez, Thomas, 1959– illustrator.
Title: Countdown : 2979 days to the moon / written by Suzanne Slade ; illustrated by Thomas Gonzalez.
Description: Atlanta : Peachtree Publishers, [2018] | Includes bibliographical references. | Audience: Ages 8–12. | Audience: Grades 4 to 6.
Identifiers: LCCN 2017060838 | ISBN 9781682630136
Subjects: LCSH: Project Apollo (U.S.)—Juvenile literature. | Space flight to the moon—History—Juvenile literature.
Classification: LCC TL789.8.U6 A581823 2018 | DDC 629.45/4—dc23 LC record available at *https://lccn.loc.gov/2017060838*

Countdown

2979 Days to the Moon

Written by Suzanne Slade
Illustrated by Thomas Gonzalez

PEACHTREE
ATLANTA

Contents

Chapter 1: A Daring Dream

At first
it's only a dream—
an ambitious, outrageous idea.

The dream seems so big,
so impossible,
that few people dare to say it out loud.

Until one day,
May 25, 1961,
one man,
President John F. Kennedy,
bravely announces the dream to the world:

"I believe that this nation should commit itself
to achieving the goal, before this decade is out,
of landing a man on the moon
and returning him safely to the earth."

But how can someone soar all the way to the Moon,
two hundred and forty-thousand miles through space?
America knows the answer: teamwork.

Thousands of engineers, technicians,
mathematicians, scientists, and machinists,
working on engines, computers, and airplanes,
join Project Apollo,
a new space program with one objective—
land a man on the Moon and bring him safely home.

But America isn't the only country
with an outrageous dream.
The Soviet Union has its own plan
to put the very first man
on the Moon.

Determined to win this Space Race,
the Apollo team begins their herculean task:
designing, building, and testing four new crafts—
each with its own important role—
that must work flawlessly together.
The command module
will carry the crew to the Moon and back.
The service module
will provide electricity, oxygen, and other supplies.
The lunar module
will land on the Moon and provide a home there.
And the mighty Saturn rocket
must launch the entire mission into space.

The president watches and waits.
His end-of-the-decade deadline
seems a long time away.
But for this lofty dream—
man's first Moon landing—
it isn't much time at all.

Still, Kennedy believes in his country,
and teamwork.

So does the smiling Texas crowd,
waving wildly during a motorcade parade
on a sunny fall day—
November 22, 1963.

Suddenly an assassin takes aim.
In an instant,
the brave voice is silenced—
the visionary gone.

But the dream remains
in hopeful hearts,
now more important than ever.

And America's quest for the Moon continues,
to honor their beloved leader,
to help heal a hurting nation,
to prove that violence doesn't destroy dreams.

"…it will not be one man going to the moon…it will be an entire nation. For all of us must work to put him there."

—President John F. Kennedy, May 25, 1961

Chapter 2
The First Mission—Apollo 1

January 27, 1967

Three men in white space suits
climb inside a gumdrop-shaped command module
on a launchpad in Florida.

Gus Grissom,
a decorated Air Force pilot and experienced astronaut,
has already flown in space—twice.

Ed White,
a born pilot who flew his first plane when he was only twelve,
took America's first space walk.

And Roger Chaffee,
the youngest of the crew—only thirty-one—
is already a top Navy pilot.

Each astronaut has different skills and experiences,
yet they have much in common.
All three were Boy Scouts many years ago.
Each has two children
and a supportive wife who silently worries
every time her husband takes to the skies.

But this afternoon, there's no need for worry.
Today is a practice countdown—
routine testing on the ground
to prepare for the historic flight of Apollo 1.

In three short weeks,
Grissom, White, and Chaffee
will blast off into space,
circle Earth,
and pave a path for future missions to the Moon.

Sitting side by side in their snug spacecraft,
the metal hatch latched tight behind them,
the astronauts focus
on hundreds of dials and gauges overhead.

But a radio problem—
loud, crackling static—
disrupts their work.

The annoying static continues for hours
and the astronauts begin to wonder:
If they can't talk to technicians
thousands of feet away,
how will they talk to Earth
from hundreds of miles up in space?
As the Florida sunset fades,
their frustration grows.

Huge floodlights snap on.
Static still crackling,
the testing continues.

Suddenly the unthinkable happens.
"Flame!" Chaffee announces.
"We've got a fire in the cockpit!" White cries.
"We have a bad fire!" Chaffee shouts.
A final shriek
echoes across the radio,
then
silence.

Engineers and technicians
stare at television monitors
in disbelief
as flames fill the spacecraft.

Feet heavy with dread,
technicians race to the launchpad.
They battle intense heat,
ferocious flames,
and choking smoke.

Finally, they pry
the searing metal hatch open.
But all inside—
Grissom, White, and Chaffee—
are lost.

An entire nation goes into shock.
Then shock turns to disbelief,
disbelief to grief.
The families,
the team,
and the country
are devastated.

How had the dream,
all the careful plans,
gone so wrong?

Is the Moon
too big a dream
after all?

"There's a lot of unknowns of course,
and a lot of problems that could develop...
and that's what we're there for...
to find out if this thing will work..."

—Roger Chaffee, December 1966

Apollo 1

Launch: scheduled for February 21, 1967; crew dies on launchpad during preflight test on January 27, 1967

★ ★

Name: Virgil Ivan "Gus" Grissom

Born: April 3, 1926

Died: January 27, 1967

Age during mission: 40

Position: Commander

Education: BS, mechanical engineering, Purdue University; BS, Air Force Institute of Technology

Military service: United States Air Force

NASA Group: 1 (1959)

Experience:

- one of the original seven Mercury astronauts
- pilot, Mercury Redstone 4
- command pilot, Gemini 3 (with John Young)
- support crew, Gemini 4
- backup crew, Gemini 6

Name: Edward Higgins White II

Born: November 14, 1930

Died: January 27, 1967

Age during mission: 36

Position: Senior Pilot

Education: BS, United States Military Academy (same class as Michael Collins); MS, aeronautical engineering, University of Michigan

Military service: United States Air Force

NASA Group: 2 (1962)

Experience:

- pilot, Gemini 4 (with James McDivitt)
- backup crew, Gemini 7

Name: Roger Bruce Chaffee

Born: February 15, 1935

Died: January 27, 1967

Age during mission: 31

Position: Pilot

Education: BS, aeronautical engineering, Purdue University

Military service: United States Navy

NASA Group: 3 (1963)

Experience:

- support crew, Gemini 3
- support crew, Gemini 4

Left: Grissom, Chaffee, and White check out the couch installation on the Apollo command module

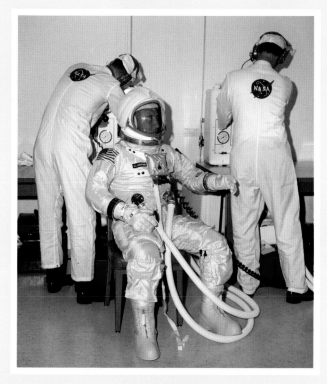

Left: Technicians help Grissom try on a space suit

Right: The Apollo 1 command module after the fire

Chapter 3: The Mission Continues

Piece by piece,
the charred Apollo 1 command module is taken apart
to find the source of that deadly blaze.

The verdict:
a tiny wire is to blame.
A spark from one frayed wire started that first, small flame.

But there are other problems too:
a heavy hatch with many bolts
that took too long to open,
and a cabin pressurized with 100 percent pure oxygen,
creating an environment where everything was flammable.

Fingers point in all directions.
The command module built to fly on Apollo 2
is grounded
forever.
NASA also decides there will never be
a mission called Apollo 3.

The team replays the tragedy
over and over.
For some,
the guilt and grief is overwhelming.

But then the team remembers
early adventurers who faced
uncharted, unpredictable oceans
to explore a mysterious, far-off land—America.

They recall the determined, smiling faces
of Grissom, White, and Chaffee,
who dreamed of exploring another new world—
one that has shared its comforting light
each dark night
for billions of years.

Their tired minds play back the haunting words
Gus Grissom said one week before the fire:

"If we die, we want people to accept it.
We're in a risky business
and we hope that if anything happens to us,
it will not delay the program.
The conquest of space is worth the risk of life."

Determined that the dream
will not die with its fallen heroes,
Team Apollo trudges on.

Engineers painstakingly redesign
the deadly command module.
They create a new hatch
that opens easily in seconds.
All wiring is completely protected
to prevent any sparks.
Everything inside the cabin, even the paint and fabric,
is now 100 percent fireproof.
And NASA passes a new edict:
no spacecraft on the launchpad
will be pressurized with pure oxygen
ever again.

Slowly,
carefully,
the Apollo program inches forward.
After much debate,
NASA changes its plan.
Upcoming missions
will be unmanned.
Before another astronaut sets one foot on a rocket,
all equipment will be thoroughly tested
on the ground
and in space.

"We would not leave the sadness behind until we accomplished what Gus Grissom, Ed White, and Roger Chaffee wanted America to do— land on the moon."

—Gene Kranz, NASA Flight director

Chapter 4: To the Sky—Apollo 4-6

November 9, 1967

After a sleepless, toss-and-turn night,
the team nervously watches
as the unmanned Apollo 4 begins its final countdown.

It will be the first flight of the new Saturn V,
the tallest, heaviest, most powerful rocket in the world.
This bold "all-up" mission will test the rocket's three stages,
each with its own engines and fuel,
that work together like a relay team—
taking turns pushing the craft into space.

Apollo 4 plans to orbit Earth,
then answer two crucial questions:
Will the command module survive
a fiery reentry into Earth's atmosphere?
Will it stay cool enough
for the astronauts to survive?
If this mission fails,
the dream of a Moon landing in three years
might never come true.

"Five, four…" The first stage ignites.
"All engines are running. We have lift-off!"
Deafening sound waves boom across the launchpad.
Miles away, tall buildings quake.
Huge glass windows rattle.
Wide-eyed, nearly tongue-tied,
the usually mild-mannered reporter Walter Cronkite
shouts into his microphone, "The roar is terrific!"

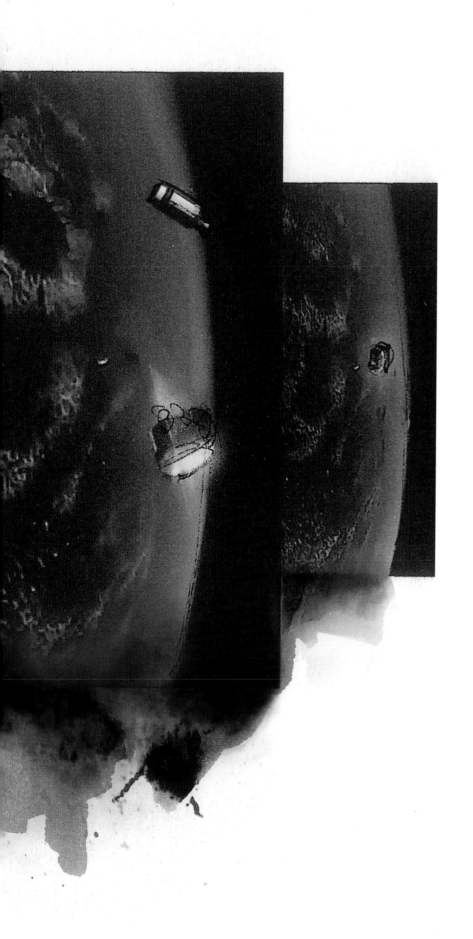

The rocket slowly rises from the ground.
The first stage finishes its fuel
and drops off into the ocean.

The team lets out a sigh of relief,
then holds their breath again.
The two remaining stages must fire—
each at the perfect moment—
to keep the rocket on the proper path.

The second stage ignites,
pushes the spacecraft
higher and faster
into the steel-blue sky,
and falls into the sea.

The third stage fires
and propels the craft into Earth orbit
right on schedule,
then shuts off.
For just a moment the team relaxes.
But the mission isn't over yet.

Apollo 4 circles Earth,
then orbits a second time.
The third stage reignites
just as planned,
and pushes the spacecraft even higher—
more than 10,000 miles above Earth.

Then comes the moment the team is waiting for—
the tiny command module hurtles home
at 25,000 miles per hour.
Its heat shield reaches a blistering 5000F.
But inside,
the temperature is only 70F,
as it splashes down in the Pacific Ocean.
The dream is still alive.

January 22, 1968

Two months later,
the next unmanned mission—Apollo 5—
soars into the sunset sky.

It's carrying the lunar module,
an important new spacecraft
designed to land on the Moon
and provide a safe home there for astronauts.
The mission's goal:
test the module's landing and launch engines
in space.

During its eleven-hour night flight,
the metal ship circles Earth four times,
and passes every major test.
Team Apollo takes another small step
toward the Moon.

April 4, 1968
Apollo 6 blasts off.
Its objective—
test the Saturn V rocket with a heavier load.
This is the first time the rocket will carry
all three crafts needed for a moon-landing mission:
command module, service module, and lunar module.

Minutes after liftoff,
the rocket starts shaking uncontrollably.

NASA calls it "pogo" vibrations,
but their ship is bouncing harder and faster
than any pogo stick.

Severe vibrations knock out one engine,
then another.
The rocket's computer fights
to keep other engines burning longer than planned
and saves the flight.

The spacecraft orbits Earth twice.
Then Mission Control discovers another problem.
The engine designed to push the ship
out of Earth orbit
and on its way to the Moon
won't ignite.
Not even a spark.

Newspapers announce Apollo 6 is a failure.
The nation's confidence is shaken.
The end of the decade deadline,
only twenty-one short months away,
seems impossible.

The next day, the Apollo team reconvenes
and creates a new plan—
a do-whatever-it-takes, work-round-the-clock plan.
Every problem on Apollo 6
is thoroughly analyzed.
Faulty systems are reviewed,
redesigned,
and retested.

Kennedy's deadline is quickly approaching.
The Space Race is heating up.
So Apollo's director makes a bold decision—
astronauts will fly the next mission.

"The Apollo program director indicated
confidence today that past problems can be
corrected and said he has recommended the
next Saturn 5[V] moon rocket be launched
with men aboard."

— *Chicago Tribune*, April 25, 1968

Apollo 4

Launch: November 9, 1967

Duration: 8 hours, 37 minutes

Rocket: Saturn V

Orbits: 3

Goal: Test all three of Saturn V's stages in an "all-up" mission

Saturn V in the Vehicle Assembly Building at the Kennedy Space Center

Apollo 5

Launch: January 22, 1968

Duration: 11 hours, 10 minutes

Rocket: Saturn IB

Orbits: 7

Goal: Test the lunar module in space

The lunar module is moved into position

Apollo 6

Launch: April 4, 1968

Duration: 9 hours, 57 minutes

Rocket: Saturn V

Orbits: 3

Goal: Test Saturn V with near-full load and launch engines

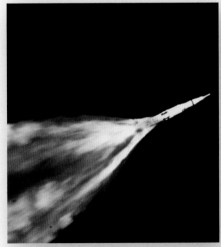

A trail of flames from the engines of Apollo 6

Left: Saturn V moving to the launchpad on the Crawler Transporter Vehicle
Right: Apollo 4 on the launchpad

Left: Mission Control
Right: Apollo 5 mission liftoff

Left: Mexico, Arizona, and the Gulf of California as seen from space
Right: Command module is hoisted aboard the USS Okinawa

Chapter 5
Risking It All—Apollo 7

October 11, 1968
Three brave astronauts—
Wally Schirra, Walt Cunningham, and Donn Eisele—
step onto Launch Pad 34,
the sacred place where Apollo 1 burned.

Silently, the crew boards the spacecraft,
remembering their close friends
who gave their lives
on this very spot.

Behind the astronauts' steadfast, smiling faces,
unwelcome thoughts creep in.
Will there be another spark
in the capsule's fifteen miles of wire?
Is this their last mission?
Their last day?

The countdown begins.
America—
and the world—
anxiously waits.

A thunderous roar wakes the sleepy Florida swamps.
Apollo 7
pulls
and strains
against Earth's gravity grip,
then finally soars
free
through the ice-blue sky,
its fiery tail glowing behind.

During their Earth orbit mission,
the astronauts will test the redesigned command module
and check out every system—
navigation, communication, and even elimination—
to prepare for longer flights to the Moon.

Soaring around Earth at 17,500 mph,
the men happily report
the command module is performing better than expected.
But the busy crew is not happy
about Mission Control's new requests—
extra duties not listed on their flight plan.

Back home,
people crowd near televisions
to watch the first live transmission from space—
fuzzy black-and-white pictures
of astronauts wearing three-day-old beards,
floating inside a cramped command module—
overworked and exhausted,
yet giddy with excitement.

Schirra holds up a sign.
"Keep those cards and letters coming in, folks."
Three smiles in space
become millions of smiles on Earth.

The next morning,
eager viewers tune in again
to *The Wally, Walt, and Donn Show.*
"Coming to you live from outer space,"
Eisele exclaims,
"the one and only original
Apollo orbiting road show…"
Soon a command module tour begins—
the food bay, sleep station,
and Cunningham demonstrating
how astronauts stay fit by pulling on ropes.

The crew circles Earth
again and again—
163 times.
They conduct dozens of tests,
make seven television appearances,
and send home hundreds
of breathtaking photos of Earth.

KEEP THOSE CARDS AND LETTERS COMING IN FOLKS

After eleven days,
it's time for the last,
critical part of the mission:
the landing.

But a seemingly small problem—
the common cold—
has become a big problem in space,
where there's little gravity to drain painful, stuffy heads.

The crew makes a surprising announcement:
no one will wear a helmet during landing.
They want to plug noses and pop ears
to keep their eardrums from bursting.

Mission Control says no.
The risk is too great.
Colds or no colds,
they must wear helmets!

The crew strongly disagrees
and decides to mutiny.

Apollo 7 splashes down
into the Atlantic Ocean
without helmets,
without injuries.

The astronauts are ecstatic to be safely home,
though they are bobbing in the salty seas,
dangling upside-down from their safety belts.

Soon, three large bags inflate
and flip the craft
right side up.

The long, tiring mission is a success.
It's time for Apollo
to head for the Moon!

"We have a magnificent flying machine
up here, but we wouldn't have been going
this long without you guys."

—Walt Cunningham to Mission Control,
October 21, 1968

Apollo 7

Launch: October 11, 1968

Splashdown: October 22, 1968

Duration: eleven days

* *

Name: Walter Marty Schirra Jr.

Born: March 12, 1923

Died: May 3, 2007

Age during mission: 45

Position: Commander

Education: BS, United States Naval Academy

Military service: United States Navy

NASA Group: 1 (1959)

Experience:

- one of the original seven Mercury astronauts

- pilot, Mercury Atlas 8

- backup crew, Gemini 3

- command pilot, Gemini 6 (with Tom Stafford); first space rendezvous between Gemini 6 and 7

- backup crew, Apollo 1

Name: Ronnie Walter Cunningham

Born: March 16, 1932

Age during mission: 36

Position: Lunar Module Pilot

Education: BA and MA, physics, University of California at Los Angeles

Military service: United States Navy and United States Marine Corps

NASA Group: 3 (1963)

Experience:

- backup crew, Apollo 1

- support crew, Gemini 8

Name: Donn F. Eisele

Born: June 23, 1930

Died: December 2, 1987

Age during mission: 37

Position: Command Module Pilot

Education: BS, United States Naval Academy; MS, astronautics, Air Force Institute of Technology

Military service: United States Air Force

NASA Group: 3 (1963)

Experience: backup crew, Apollo 1

Top left: The erection of the first stage of Apollo 7's Saturn IB rocket.

Top right: The Apollo 7 crew on the deck of the NASA Motor Vessel Retriever. Left to right: Cunningham, Eisele, Schirra.

Bottom: Apollo 7 launches from the Kennedy Space Center's Launch Complex 34

Chapter 6: Aiming for the Moon—Apollo 8

December 21, 1968
Two months later,
another rocket rumbles on the launchpad.

The goal of Apollo 8 seems simple—
orbit the Moon and return home.
But the mission is incredibly complicated
and dangerous.
No one has ever traveled all the way to the Moon.

In a complex rocket ship made of five million parts,
one little defect,
one tiny problem,
could end everything.

Among the thousands gathered,
legendary pilot Charles Lindbergh,
the man who made the first solo flight across the Atlantic,
stands waiting—anticipating.
He's come to witness
Frank Borman, Jim Lovell, and Bill Anders
begin their historic first flight to the Moon.

Explosive fire. Deafening noise.
The rocket blasts off
above an inferno of white-hot flames.
The powerful force of 4 g's
press Borman, Lovell, and Anders
deep into their seats
while they wonder if they'll see their wives,
their precious children,
again.

Thirsty rocket engines
drink thousands of gallons of fuel each second,
catapulting the craft
on its way into space.

The rocket's first stage finishes its fuel,
then falls into the sea.
The second stage continues pushing the craft
higher and faster,
before breaking away and splashing into the ocean.
The third stage takes over,
sending Borman, Lovell, and Anders into Earth orbit,
then shuts off for a short rest.

Quietly circling Earth,
the astronauts remove gloves and helmets,
making it easier to operate their controls
in "parking orbit."

Two hours later,
Mission Control announces,
"Apollo 8. You are Go for TLI,"
giving them permission for Trans-Lunar Injection—
a propulsion burst that will push their spacecraft
out of Earth orbit
on its trajectory to the Moon.

The men steal a last glance at their beautiful home,
then Borman begins the TLI countdown: "9, 8, 7..."
With each passing second,
excitement builds at Mission Control.
No astronaut—American or Soviet—
has ridden a rocket beyond Earth orbit.
"3, 2, light On. Ignition," Borman announces.
"Ignition," Lovell confirms.
The third-stage engine reignites,
sending the craft on its long trek to the Moon.

As Apollo 8 screams into space,
Borman, Lovell, and Anders
become the first humans
to fly above Earth orbit.

Hour after hour,
the astronauts coast through blackness,
cold nothingness,
space.

On December 22,
the crew starts their first television transmission.
Mesmerized Earth viewers
watch Lovell fix a snack in space.
"He is making up a bag of chocolate pudding,"
Borman explains with a smile.

Minutes later, Lovell floats by the camera again.
"Happy Birthday, Mother," he says,
sending her a special greeting from space.

Outside their window,
the Earth shrinks
from a basketball,
to a baseball,
to a golf ball.

But the astronauts can't see the Moon—
not even a glimpse.
The entire trip,
their ship has been flying tail-first,
its windows facing home.

About 39,000 miles from their destination,
the Moon's gravity begins pulling them
faster
and closer
to its mysterious, gray surface.

Sixty-six hours after leaving home,
it's finally time.
The astronauts must fly around the far side of the Moon,
where communication with Earth will be impossible,
and put their ship into lunar orbit.

Mission Control signs off: "Safe journey, guys."
"We'll see you on the other side," Lovell promises.
Then the radio goes silent.

Now the team can only wait,
hoping Lovell keeps his promise.

Minutes later,
Lovell spies what he's been waiting for.
"Hey, I got the Moon," he says. "Right below us."
"Oh, my God!" Anders exclaims,
realizing that the dark lines outside his window
are mountains on the Moon!
"All right, all right, come on," Borman barks.
"You're going to look at that for a long time."
The crew quickly refocuses
and prepares for a short engine burn
to slow their craft
so the Moon's gravity can pull them into lunar orbit.

If the engine doesn't start,
their ship will whip around the Moon
and career toward home.
If the engine shuts down early,
they could soar into an unplanned orbit.
But if the engine runs too long,
they'll crash into the Moon.

The men meticulously complete each item on the checklist.
Then Lovell fires the engine.
Its powerful thrust slows the metal craft
more than 1,000 mph in only four minutes.
"Shutdown," Borman announces.
The burn is a success. Apollo 8 is in lunar orbit!

The astronauts peer outside.
Sixty-nine miles below,
they spy a secret land no human eye has ever seen—
the far side of the Moon.
A place of utter desolation
filled with colossal craters and mighty mountains.

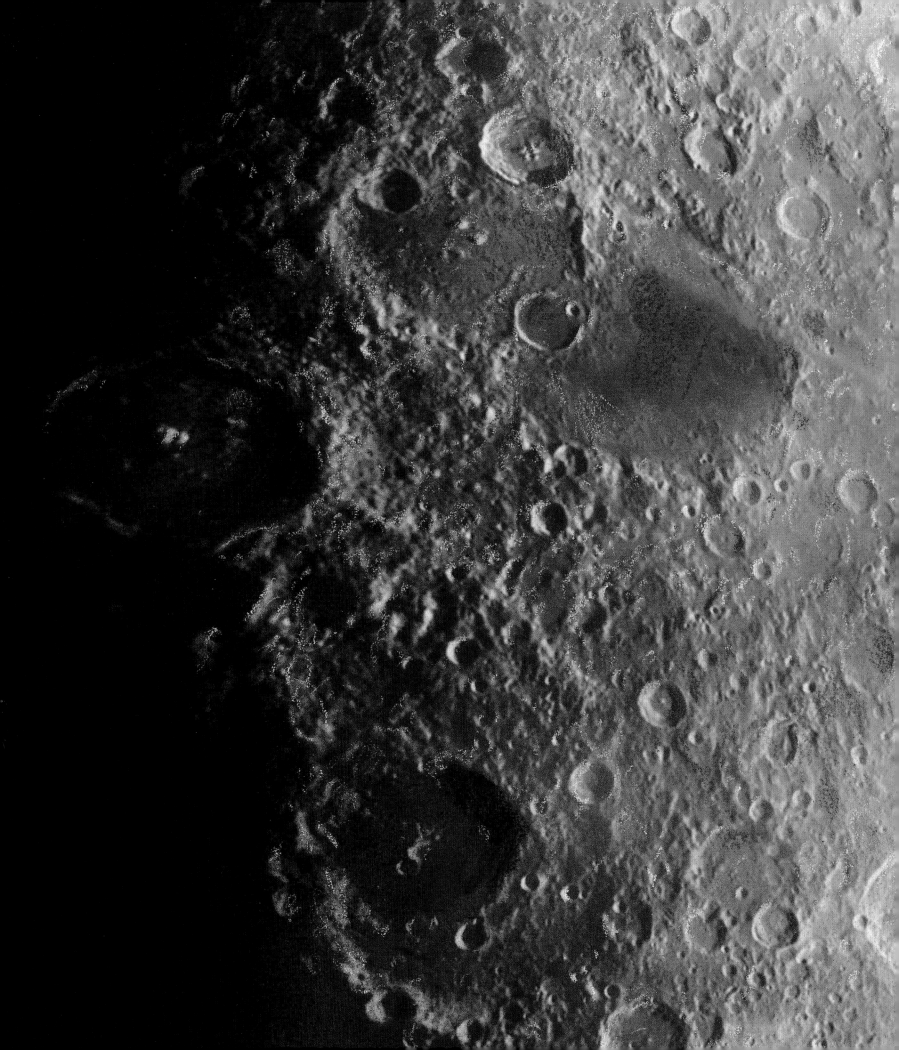

After thirty-four minutes of radio silence
Mission Control calls out to the crew,
"Apollo 8, Houston. Over."
No answer.

Mission Control radios again.
And again.
And again.

"Go ahead, Houston," Lovell finally replies.
"This is Apollo 8. Burn complete."
"Good to hear your voice," Mission Control responds.

Back home, the astronauts' wives
are also thrilled to hear Lovell's voice
coming from their cherished squawk boxes—
small speakers provided by NASA
that transmit every mission conversation
into their living rooms.

"What does the ole Moon look like…?" Mission Control asks.
The wives lean in close to their squawk boxes
while Lovell tries to find Earth words
to describe the strange land.
"Like plaster of Paris," he replies, "…a grayish beach sand."

The tiny craft orbits the Moon
again and again,
while the astronauts study the gray surface below.
Anders photographs ancient craters and lonely mountains.
Then he spots something surprising,
almost surreal.

A brilliant blue ball,
wrapped in wispy white cotton,
rising above the stark horizon.
Earthrise on Christmas Eve, 1968.
Anders grabs a camera
and takes a picture of the sparkling jewel.

Their ship continues sailing around the Moon,
ten laps in all.
Then the critical moment of the mission arrives.
The rocket engine must reignite
and push the craft out of lunar orbit.
If it fails, the men will be trapped in space
forever.

The spacecraft silently slips around the far side of the Moon,
losing all communication with Earth again
while the crew prepares for reignition.

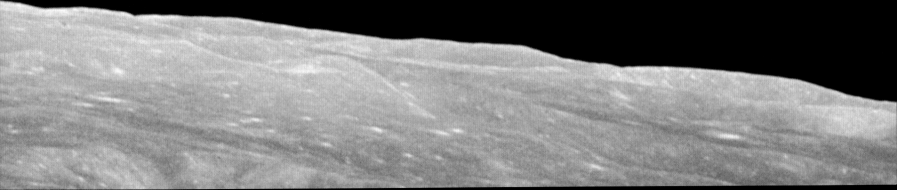

Mission Control
and the world
must wait twelve seemingly endless minutes
to learn the astronauts' fate.

The first sound they hear
that Christmas day
is Lovell's voice from a quarter million miles away.
"Please be informed there is a Santa Claus!"

The engine fired.
The men are coming home.

"From the crew of Apollo 8, we close with good night,
good luck, a Merry Christmas and God bless all of you—
all of you on the good Earth."

—Frank Borman, Christmas Day 1968

Apollo 8

Launch: December 21, 1968

Splashdown: December 27, 1968

Duration: six days

★ ★

Name: Frank Borman

Born: March 14, 1928

Age during mission: 40

Position: Commander

Education: BS, United States Military Academy; MS, aeronautical engineering, California Institute of Technology

Military service: United States Air Force

NASA Group: 2 (1962)

Experience:

- backup crew, Gemini 4
- command pilot, Gemini 7 (with Jim Lovell)

Name: William A. Anders

Born: October 17, 1933

Age during mission: 35

Position: Lunar Module Pilot

Education: BS, United States Naval Academy; MS, nuclear engineering, Air Force Institute of Technology

Military service: United States Air Force

NASA Group: 3 (1963)

Experience: backup crew, Gemini 11

Name: James A. Lovell

Born: March 25, 1928

Age during mission: 40

Position: Command Module Pilot

Education: BS, United States Naval Academy

Military service: United States Navy

NASA Group: 2 (1962)

Experience:

- backup crew, Gemini 4
- pilot, Gemini 7 (with Frank Borman)
- support crew, Gemini 8
- backup crew, Gemini 9
- command pilot, Gemini 12 (with Buzz Aldrin)

Left: The final assembly of the Saturn V launch vehicle

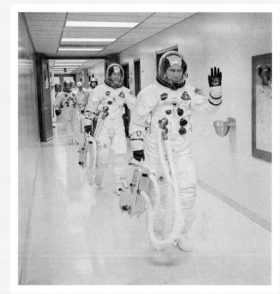

Above: Borman, Lovell, and Anders head to the launchpad

Left: More than 2,000 people welcome the Apollo 8 crew back home

Chapter 7: Spider in Space—Apollo 9

March 3, 1969
After an official launch-day breakfast—
scrambled eggs, steak, toast, and orange juice—
James McDivitt, Dave Scott, and Rusty Schweickart
suit up,
strap in,
and hurtle toward space
carrying a new craft—the lunar module named Spider.
It's specially designed to land on the Moon
and provide a home there for astronauts.

But this mission isn't going to the Moon.
Its objective—
test the lunar module while orbiting Earth.

The Apollo 9 crew also has another dangerous assignment:
wear a new suit and backpack
in the vacuum of space
for the very first time.

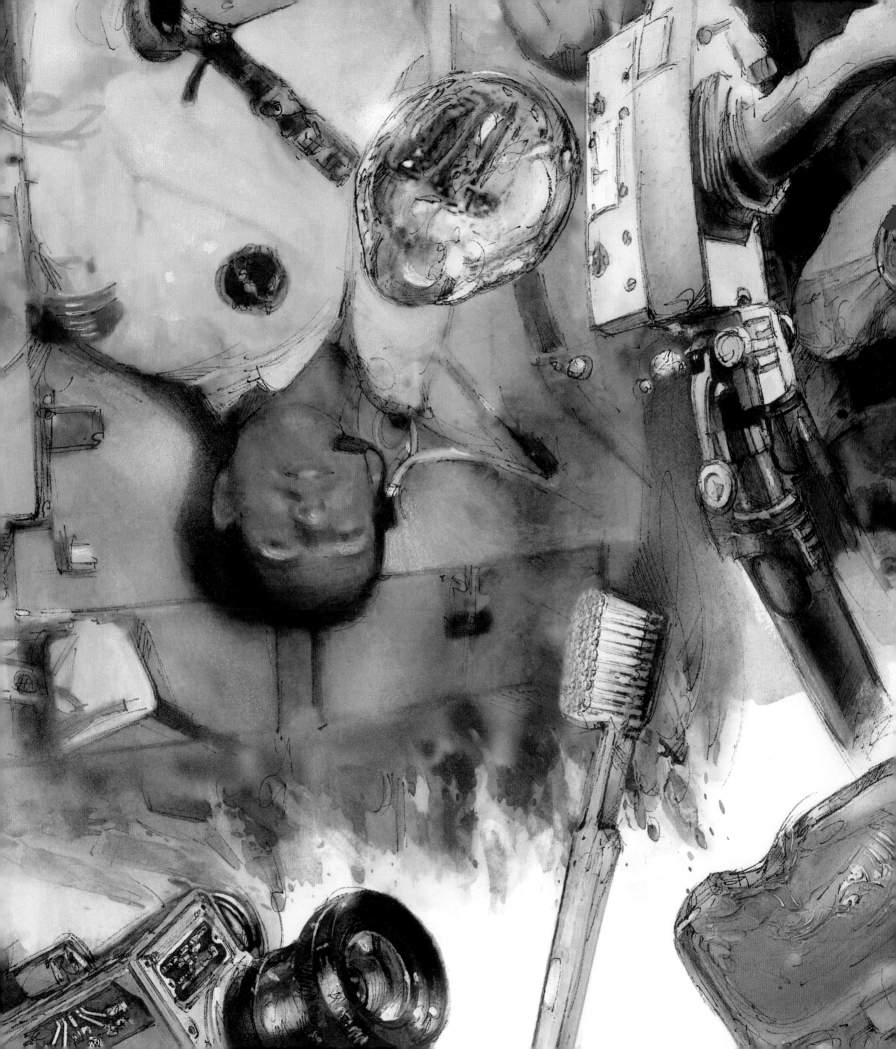

As the ship enters Earth orbit,
experienced astronauts McDivitt and Scott
enjoy the weightlessness of space,
where upside down feels like right side up,
and lost cameras, toothbrushes, and dried-food pouches
play hide-and-seek
with crew who forgot to velcro them in place.

But the fun doesn't last long for Schweickart,
a first-time space traveler.
He soon discovers that
weightlessness upsets his stomach,
floating vomit isn't easy to catch,
and getting a simple drink of water
is a challenging game of "capture the droplets."

On the fourth day,
Schweickart puts on the new space suit,
opens the hatch,
and steps outside onto the ship's platform.
He trusts the suit will keep him safe
and its backpack will supply the oxygen he needs
in the vast vacuum of space.

While Scott repairs the movie camera
so he can film this space adventure,
Schweickart marvels at the majestic sight—
breathtaking blue swirls below
and velvety black sky above.

Then the space walk begins.
Holding tightly to handrails,
Schweickart moves around the outside the craft,
checking the suit's mobility and communication system.

After thirty-four minutes,
Schweickart crawls back inside.
His successful space walk
proves the suit is ready for a moonwalk.
But there's little time
for the busy Apollo 9 crew
to celebrate.

The next morning,
the lunar module test begins.
With its four spindly legs,
two triangle bug-eye windows,
and dozens of antennae,
the lunar module called Spider
took seven years to build.

But will it protect its passengers
in the harsh conditions of space?
McDivitt and Schweickart
are ready to risk their lives to find out.

The two astronauts board the lunar module,
while Scott stays behind to pilot the command module.
Joystick in hand, Scott carefully releases Spider
and his friends
into the blackness of space.

The astronauts fire Spider's engine.
Finally on its own,
the lunar module and its crew float away
into the silent, starless sea.

Apollo 9

Launch: March 3, 1969

Splashdown: March 13, 1969

Duration: ten days

★ ★

Name: James A. McDivitt

Born: June 10, 1929

Age during mission: 40

Position: Commander

Education: BS, aeronautical engineering, University of Michigan

Military service: United States Air Force

NASA Group: 2 (1962)

Experience:

- command pilot, Gemini 4 (with Ed White)
- backup crew, Apollo 1

Name: Russell L. Schweickart

Born: October 25, 1935

Age during mission: 34

Position: Lunar Module Pilot

Education: BS and MS, aeronautical engineering, Massachusetts Institute of Technology

Military service: United States Air Force

NASA Group: 3 (1963)

Experience:

- research scientist at the Experimental Astronomy Laboratory of the Massachusetts Institute of Technology
- backup crew, Apollo 1

Name: David R. Scott

Born: June 6, 1932

Age during mission: 37

Position: Command Module Pilot

Education: BS, United States Military Academy; MS, aeronautics and astronautics, Massachusetts Institute of Technology

Military service: United States Air Force

NASA Group: 3 (1963)

Experience:

- pilot, Gemini 8 (with Neil Armstrong)
- backup crew, Apollo 1

Top left: The Apollo 9 crew.
Left to right: McDivitt,
Scott, Schweickart.

Top right: The Mission Operations
Control Room, during a live
television transmission of Apollo 9
as it orbits Earth

Left: Schweickart stands on
the lunar module porch during
his space walk

Chapter 8
Dress Rehearsal—
Apollo 10

May 18, 1969
Warm Florida winds blow 19 knots,
as three explorers blast off for the heavens.

Like the astronauts before them,
Tom Stafford, John Young, and Gene Cernan
have trained for many years,
waited their whole lives
for launch day.

Their assignment—
fly a lunar module mere miles from the Moon
and scout the landing site
to prepare for the next mission,
the first Moon landing.

Two and a half hours after kissing Earth good-bye,
Apollo 10 starts an engine burn to move out of Earth orbit.
Three minutes later,
the astronauts' seats begin vibrating violently.
The entire ship is shaking.
A strange buzzing noise fills the cabin—
a sound the crew has never heard before.
Yet, deep down they all know what it means.
The rocket has a serious problem.
They may have to abort the flight.

"We're getting small high-frequency vibrations.
Nothing to worry about,"
Stafford informs Mission Control,
hoping his reassuring words make the problem disappear.
His left hand is on the abort handle,
ready to end the mission,
but he can't bring himself to do it.
Not yet.

Stafford's eyes dart to the velocity readout.
Just as he hoped, their speed is increasing.
If he can hold out a little longer
his rattling craft might reach 24,000 mph,
the speed it needs to leave its Earth orbit
and head to the Moon.

Second by second,
the determined crew hangs on.
Faster and faster,
their vibrating vessel accelerates
for sixty nerve-wracking seconds.

Finally, they make it—24,000 mph.
In an instant, the engine turns off.
The buzzing and shaking stops.
The mission is still a go.
Apollo 10 is on its way to the Moon!

Stafford, Young, and Cernan coast
through deep space
for three days,
testing, navigating, eating, and sleeping.

In their few free moments,
they listen to favorite sounds from Earth
on a floating cassette tape player.
Frank Sinatra's smooth voice croons a familiar tune,
"Fly Me to the Moon."

As the astronauts sing along,
the cramped, cozy capsule
almost feels like home.

Soon Apollo 10 flies into lunar orbit
and begins circling the Moon.
Its camera sends home the first color TV transmission
of the mysterious, rocky land.

Thousands of people on Earth
become space voyagers,
exploring an uncharted, alien land
up close.

"We should be coming right
over the Smyth's Sea," Cernan explains.
A dark area that from Earth looks like an ocean
looms across television screens.
Curious viewers stare in awe.
The "sea" is an enormous, dusty plain!

Next, brilliant white spots appear in the grayish brown soil.
Stafford explains to his audience back home
that they are small, young craters.

Then the mighty Langrenus comes into view—
an ancient crater over a mile deep
with one towering peak in its center.

But much too soon, the camera turns off,
leaving inquisitive earthlings
longing for more.

On the fourth day,
the main scouting operation begins.
Young pilots the command module
while Stafford and Cernan board the lunar module, Snoopy.
Their goals—
investigate the landing target for the next Moon mission
and test out Snoopy.

"Have a good time while we're gone," Cernan calls
as the astronauts steer Snoopy
from the safety of the command module.
Soon they cruise over the far side of the Moon
less than nine miles from the cratered surface.

Stafford and Cernan soar closer to the Moon
than any human has ever been.
So close
they feel as if they can almost touch its dusty mountaintops.

Eyes fixed on the gray surface,
they search for Apollo 11's proposed landing site—
the Sea of Tranquility—
a special lava formation created millions of years ago.

Then Stafford and Cernan see it—
a round, smooth "lake" without a single drop of water.
Stafford reports back to Mission Control.
The Sea of Tranquility looks smooth,
just as they'd hoped—
the perfect place
for the next crew to land on the Moon.

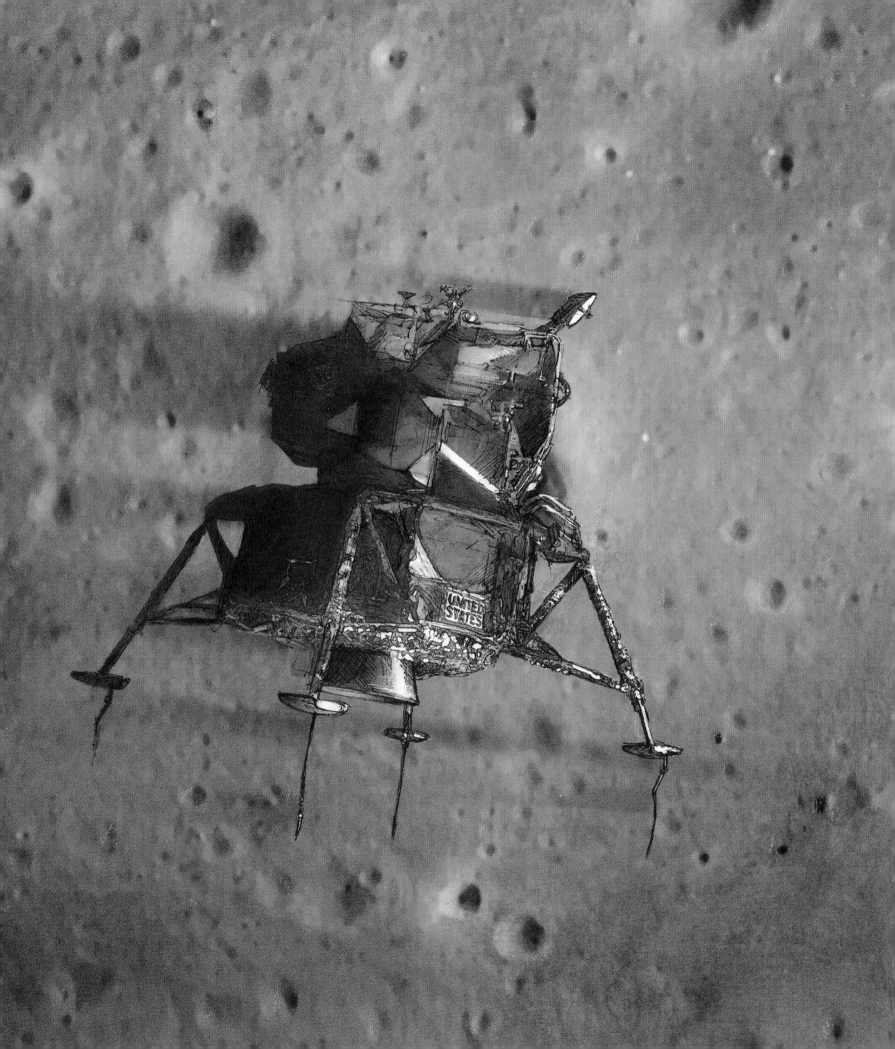

Stafford and Cernan fly onward,
testing Snoopy, taking pictures,
and studying the Moon's uneven gravity.
Soon, stomachs start to growl.
The astronauts add water to food packs
and dine on chicken and fruit cocktail.

An hour later,
Snoopy suddenly spins out of control,
around and around.
No one knows that one switch is in the wrong position—
an error in the flight-plan checklist.

Stafford's mind spins like the metal craft.
He can't afford to panic.
Hoping his first instinct is correct,
Stafford presses a button
that releases a heavy piece of equipment—
Snoopy's descent engine—
to lighten his craft
and make it easier to get under control.
Then he fires the rocket thrusters
and gets Snoopy flying right again.

Shaken,
the astronauts remind themselves—
they must always stay alert.
One simple mistake
at any time
could end the mission
and their lives.

Their duties completed,
Stafford and Cernan check their navigation system,
then search the ink-black horizon
for the command module.

In the distance,
they spot a warm, welcoming light
Snoopy glides toward it,
and safely docks.

The dress rehearsal is a success.
Apollo 11 is clear to attempt the first Moon landing!

"One thing about working 24 hours a day,
we've got a beautiful view up here."

—Tom Stafford, May 19, 1969

Apollo 10

Launch: May 18, 1969

Splashdown: May 26, 1969

Duration: eight days

★ ★

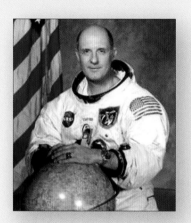

Name: Thomas R. Stafford

Born: September 17, 1930

Age during mission: 38

Position: Commander

Education: BS, United States Naval Academy

Military service: United States Air Force

NASA Group: 2 (1962)

Experience:

- backup crew, Gemini 3
- command pilot, Gemini 6 (with Wally Schirra); first space rendezvous between Gemini 6 and 7
- command pilot, Gemini 9 (with Eugene Cernan)
- backup crew, Apollo 7

Name: Eugene Andrew Cernan

Born: March 14, 1934

Died: January 16, 2017

Age during mission: 35

Position: Lunar Module Pilot

Education: BS, electrical engineering, Purdue University; MS, aeronautical engineering, United States Naval Academy

Military service: United States Navy

NASA Group: 3 (1963)

Experience:

- support crew, Gemini 4
- support crew, Gemini 7
- pilot, Gemini 9 (with Tom Stafford)
- backup crew, Gemini 12
- backup crew, Apollo 7

Name: John Watts Young

Born: September 24, 1930

Died: January 5, 2018

Age during mission: 38

Position: Command Module Pilot

Education: BS, aeronautical engineering, Georgia Institute of Technology

Military service: United States Navy

NASA Group: 2 (1962)

Experience:

- pilot, Gemini 3 (with Gus Grissom)
- backup crew, Gemini 6
- commander, Gemini 10 (with Michael Collins)
- backup crew, Apollo 7

Top left: Apollo 10, on a crawler-transporter, on the way to Pad B, Launch Complex 39, Kennedy Space Center

Top right: The flight director's console in the Mission Operations Control Room, on the first day of the Apollo 10 lunar orbit mission

Bottom: The Apollo 10 crew at the Kennedy Space Center for preflight training. Left to right: Cernan, Young, Stafford.

Chapter 9
Achieving the Dream—Apollo 11

July 16, 1969
Hours before blastoff,
the countdown begins.

"This is Apollo Saturn Launch Control.
T minus 2 hours, 34 minutes, 44 seconds and counting.
The spacecraft Commander Neil Armstrong
now aboard the Apollo 11 spacecraft."

"T minus 2 hours, 30 minutes, 55 seconds and counting....
the Command Module Pilot, astronaut Michael Collins,
who'll be sitting on the right-hand side of the spacecraft
during lift-off, boarded the spacecraft."

"T minus 2 hours, 23 minutes, 46 seconds and counting....
logged at 7:07am Eastern Daylight Time
when astronaut Buzz Aldrin boarded the spacecraft."

"T minus 1 hour, 30 minutes, 55 seconds and counting.
All elements are Go with the countdown...
aimed at landing two astronauts on the Moon."

Every eye,
every camera lens
focuses on the rumbling rocket ship,
its final seconds on Earth
slipping away.

"10, 9, ignition sequence starts…"
Fuel and liquid oxygen pour into combustion chambers.

"6, 5, 4…"
Huge rocket engines ignite and roar.

"3, 2, 1…"
Powerful flames explode on Launch Pad 39A.

"Zero…"
The ground trembles.
Thick white clouds surround the rocket.

"LIFT-OFF!"

Thousands stand spellbound.
A six-million-pound rocket,
Saturn V,
is pushing a 48-ton spacecraft
off the ground!

As the world watches the unbelievable sight,
the astronauts closely watch
the rocket's direction and rotation—
pitch, roll, and yaw.
Any errors
and the flight will be aborted,
the command module and its crew
hurled into the sea.

Twelve crucial minutes tick by.
The mighty craft enters Earth orbit
and circles the globe.
Then an engine fires,
sending the astronauts on their trajectory to the Moon.

The ship zips through space for two days and nights
while the crew stays busy with lunar module inspections,
TV transmissions, and navigation corrections
to ensure they stay on course.

On the morning of the third day,
Mission Control wakes the astronauts.
"Apollo 11, Apollo 11, this is Houston. Over."
Aldrin answers the distant voice from Texas:
"Good morning, Houston. Apollo 11."

The crew spies a breathtaking view out their window:
blue and white swirls
over rich, red sand—
Africa.

After seventy-six hours in flight,
the astronauts fire an engine
to slow their ship,
allowing the Moon's gravity to grab the spacecraft
and pull it into lunar orbit.

A massive cratered surface fills their tiny hatch window.
Armstrong gets his first glimpse of the landing approach
to the Sea of Tranquility.
He compares the rugged terrain
to his memory of photos from other missions.
"It looks very much like the pictures," he explains,
"like the difference between
watching a real football game
and one on TV."

Sunday, July 20—
after a fitful night of little sleep,
Armstrong, Collins, and Aldrin wake early,
excited and hopeful,
determined not to let Team Apollo down.

On the small blue ball thousands of miles away,
people are praying for the crew's safety—
in homes,
in churches,
even in the White House.

In Texas,
three wives wait,
hoping their husbands survive the day

Aldrin and Armstrong step into their space suits,
click on helmets and gloves,
and board their lunar module, Eagle.

Collins remains in the command module—
alone,
hoping he won't have to return to Earth alone.
Then he pushes a button
and releases Eagle.

"Okay, there you go. Beautiful!" Collins calls out
as the ships slowly drift apart.
"The Eagle has wings," Armstrong announces.

Aldrin and Armstrong have practiced
hundreds of Moon landings
in a simulator on Earth.
But now, approaching the Moon,
which has one-sixth of the gravity on Earth,
things are much different.
Unpredictable.
Real.

Eagle has enough fuel for only one trip to the Moon.
Aldrin and Armstrong have one chance
in the next twelve minutes
to lower their craft fifty thousand feet
and land.

The astronauts begin their descent
toward the stark, barren surface.
Eagle's metal feet
reach
for the Moon.
Every second its computer
makes hundreds of calculations—
hundreds of decisions—
to control the vehicle's direction and speed.

Armstrong peers through his window,
searching for lunar landmarks
to make sure they're on the right path.
Aldrin does his own double-checking,
comparing the computer's height calculations
with radar readings.
The crew can't afford any mistakes
by computers
or humans.

Eagle drifts
closer,
closer,
to the soft gray surface—
40,000 feet,
35,000 feet—
then a warning alarm sounds.

"Program Alarm," Armstrong reports.
His trained eyes dart to controls and dials,
but he can't find the problem.

The computer flashes a warning.
"It's a 1202," Armstrong informs Mission Control.
He's never seen this alarm in a simulator.
Not once.
"What is it?" he asks Aldrin.
But he gets no response.

Fear slithers in.
Will they crash?
Will they have to abort?
Will they be able to return home?

Seconds feel like hours,
as they wait for Mission Control's orders.
The men can't imagine the mission ending now.
Not after getting this close.
Not after so many people have sacrificed so much.

"We're Go on that alarm," Mission Control reports,
giving them permission to continue,
but not wasting precious seconds to explain
that an overloaded computer caused the alarm.

Sighs of relief.
The descent continues.
Eyes fixed on his computer,
Aldrin monitors their altitude:
20,000 feet,
10,000 feet,
5,000 feet.
Every second
they move 100 feet closer to the Moon.

"Eagle, you're looking great,"
says a steady voice from Mission Control.
but every heart in that Texas control room
is racing—
every person
barely breathing.
They know anything can happen
in the next few seconds.

Aldrin calls out the altitude
to make sure there are no mistakes:
"3,000 feet."
"2,000 feet."
Armstrong peers out the window,
finally able to examine the landing target,
the Sea of Tranquility,
up close.
But he doesn't like what he sees—
a giant crater
lined with huge, sharp boulders.

Armstrong turns off the automatic steering
and takes over the controls.
Carefully, he guides Eagle down
300…200…100 feet.
Eagle's engine blows powdery dust
everywhere.
Armstrong squints and strains
to see through the gray swirling cloud,
searching for a smooth, safe place to land.

A red warning light flashes.
Their landing fuel is almost gone.
"Sixty seconds," warns Mission Control.
They must land in sixty seconds or abort.
Aldrin reports their altitude, "40 feet…30 feet."
"Thirty seconds," barks Mission Control.

Heart beating twice its normal speed,
Armstrong grips the controls.
The landing has to be perfect.
One mistake, one rock,
could turn the lunar module sideways.
Eagle *must* land on its feet
or the astronauts can never leave the Moon.

Dust flying, heart pounding,
Armstrong maneuvers Eagle
down
down
down
until its feet
touch the ground.
"The Eagle has landed," Armstrong announces.

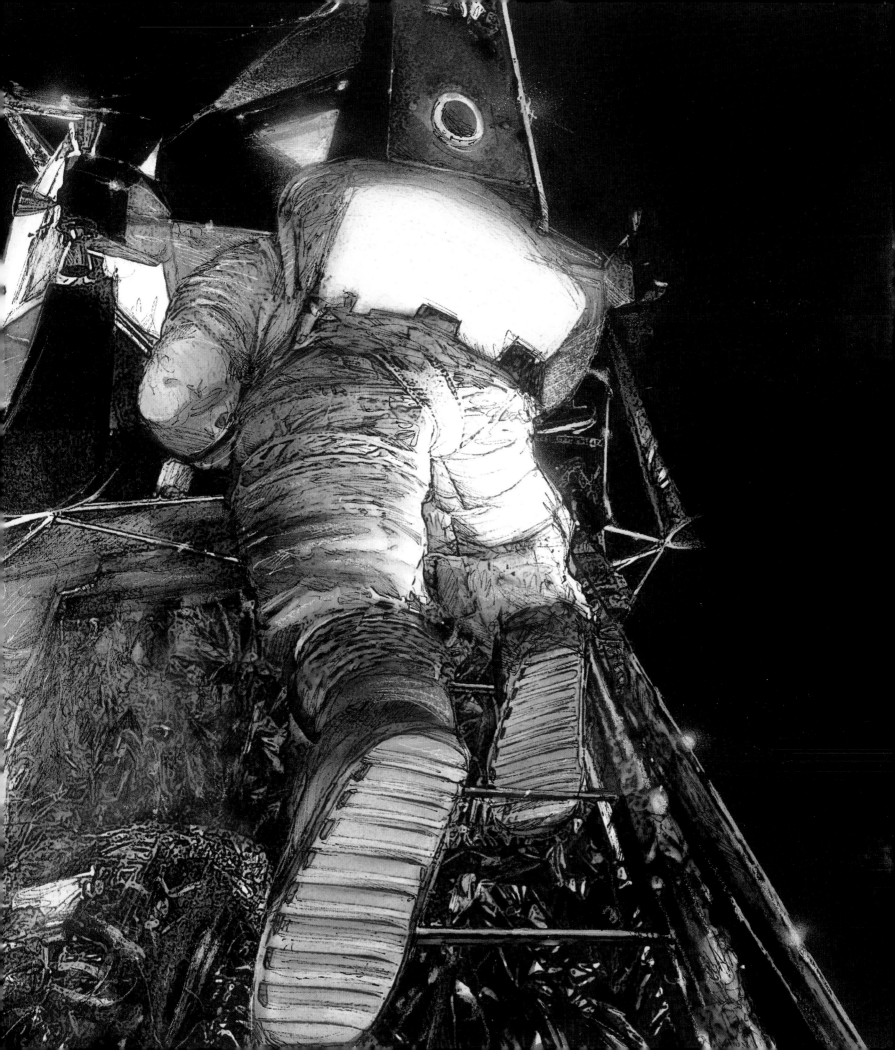

Two thousand nine hundred and seventy-nine days
after Kennedy's proclamation,
Armstrong steps onto the Moon,
leaving a footprint that will last forever.
"That's one small step for man,
one giant leap for mankind," he says.

Six hundred million people
around the world
stare at television screens in silent disbelief
as Armstrong bounds across the Moon
in slow-motion, straight-legged hops.

"Are you ready for me to come out?" Aldrin asks,
before heading down the ladder.
Three feet above the ground,
he jumps from the last rung.
"Beautiful view!" he exclaims.

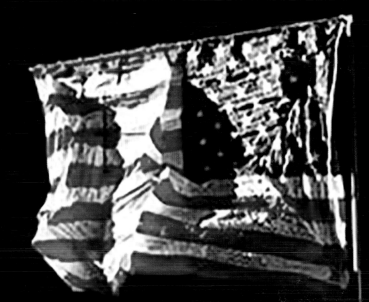

But the elated visitors have much more to do
than take in the outstanding view.
Their strict flight plan
allows only two and a half hours on the surface—
barely enough time
to complete the jobs on their checklists.

So they get right to work,
gathering rocks,
taking pictures,
conducting experiments,
planting the American flag,
and answering a call from President Nixon.
Then much too soon
their time is almost up.

With only minutes left on the Moon,
Armstrong and Aldrin remember one last job—
a task not found on any checklist.

Aldrin reaches into his pocket,
pulls out a special patch
bearing the names of the Apollo 1 astronauts—
Gus Grissom, Ed White, and Roger Chaffee—
and places it on the Moon.

Two thousand nine hundred and seventy-nine days—
the journey to the Moon was long and treacherous.
Yet through many trials, tragedies, and triumphs,
the Apollo team—
400,000 men and women—
never gave up.
Together,
they made the dream
come true.

"For one priceless moment in the whole history of
man, all the people on this Earth are truly one; one
in their pride in what you have done, and one in our
prayers that you will return safely to Earth."

—President Richard M. Nixon,
to Aldrin and Armstrong on the Moon, July 20, 1969

Apollo 11

Launch: July 16, 1969

Moon landing: July 20, 1969

Splashdown: July 24, 1969

Duration: eight days

* *

Name: Neil A. Armstrong

Born: August 5, 1930

Died: August 25, 2012

Age during mission: 38

Position: Commander

Education: BS, aeronautical engineering, Purdue University; MS, aerospace engineering, University of Southern California

Military service: United States Navy

NASA Group: 2 (1962)

Experience:

- command pilot, Gemini 8 (with David Scott)
- support crew, Gemini 10
- backup crew, Gemini 11
- backup crew, Apollo 8

Name: Edwin Eugene "Buzz" Aldrin

Born: January 20, 1930

Age during mission: 38

Position: Lunar Module Pilot

Education: BS, United States Military Academy; PhD, astronautics, Massachusetts Institute of Technology

Military service: United States Air Force

NASA Group: 3 (1963)

Experience:

- backup crew, Gemini 9
- pilot, Gemini 12 (with Jim Lovell)
- backup crew, Apollo 8

Name: Michael Collins

Born: October 31, 1930

Age during mission: 38

Position: Command Module Pilot

Education: BS, United States Military Academy (same class as Ed White)

Military service: United States Air Force

NASA Group: 3 (1963)

Experience:

- backup crew, Gemini 7
- pilot, Gemini 10 (with John Young)

Top left: The Apollo 11 command and service module

Bottom left: Armstrong performs lunar module simulations

Right: Aldrin explores the Moon. A small image of Armstrong taking the photo is reflected on Aldrin's visor.

On May 25, 1961, President John F. Kennedy announced his dream of putting a man on the Moon "before this decade is out," which meant NASA had less than nine years to achieve this feat. Building off of two earlier space programs, Project Mercury and Project Gemini, Project Apollo aimed to land astronauts on the Moon! To accomplish this ambitious goal, NASA needed thousands of workers to join Apollo's team: engineers, researchers, technicians, welders, electricians, quality inspectors, assemblers, seamstresses, and other experts.

In 1962 Team Apollo decided to use Lunar-Orbit Rendezvous (LOR) for their Moon landing mission. This bold plan involved a Saturn rocket that would carry a command module, service module, and lunar module into Earth orbit. Next, an engine would fire and push the entire craft on its trajectory to the Moon. As it neared the Moon, the spacecraft would move into lunar orbit. Finally, the lunar module would undock from the command module and land on the Moon.

Designing, building, and testing a rocket and three spacecraft was an enormous undertaking. So NASA hired companies called contractors to help. Contractors, in turn, hired subcontractors to supply components they needed.

Wernher von Braun and Arthur Rudolph, two engineers at the Marshall Space Flight Center, designed the mighty Saturn V rocket. It was so large and complicated that different

Command/service module

contractors helped create various parts, including Boeing (rocket's first stage), North American Aviation (second stage), Douglas Aircraft Company (third stage), and IBM (instrument unit with computer, guidance system, and other electronics.)

North American Aviation won the contract to build the command and service modules.

NASA hired Grumman Aircraft Engineering Corporation to build the lunar module, while subcontractors supplied various parts. TRW Space Technology Labs made the descent engine it needed to land.

Apollo space suit and PLSS backpack

flexible so an astronaut could walk and work. Hamilton Standard helped design the suit's cooling system (basically water-cooled long underwear.) They also engineered a backpack called Primary Life Support System (PLSS), with oxygen and other supplies.

The Apollo team also included many other specialists. Mathematicians plotted flight trajectories. Chemists designed fuels for the rocket and spacecraft engines. Programmers wrote code for computers that guided the crafts and identified problems. Communication experts created cameras and receivers to transmit footage from astronauts to televisions on Earth. Geologists trained astronauts so they could identify and collect certain moon rocks. Nutritionists created dried meals to keep the crew healthy. Doctors monitored their health before, during, and after missions.

Bell Aerosystems provided the ascent engine to launch the lunar module from the Moon. MIT researchers developed the navigation system.

ILC Dover created a space suit so the astronauts could safely explore the Moon. The suit worked like a one-person spaceship. It provided a safe internal pressure and protection from the sun's strong UV rays and searing 200F temperatures, yet was

At its peak, Team Apollo employed 400,000 people from across the country, all striving to land the first human on the Moon. To meet this challenge in such a short time, team members often made personal sacrifices. They worked long days, which meant missing family dinners, vacations, holiday celebrations, and precious time with their children. Despite many setbacks, sleepless nights, and surprises, Team Apollo's dedication never wavered. They kept working—together—to achieve the dream.

Bringing Apollo 11 Home

Landing the first man on the Moon was a colossal achievement, but bringing the crew safely back home was also complicated and dangerous. After their historic moonwalk, Buzz Aldrin and Neil Armstrong returned to Eagle, the lunar module, and celebrated over a late dinner. That night, the temperature in Eagle grew much colder than the astronauts expected. Armstrong didn't sleep a wink, while Aldrin managed only a few hours of restless napping.

The next morning, the astronauts prepared for the first-ever launch from the Moon. Though a lunar module ascent engine had been tested while floating in space, no one knew for sure if it would launch Eagle and its two weary passengers from the Moon.

On July 21, 1969, Aldrin began the moon launch countdown, "9, 8, 7, 6, 5…" Right on cue, the engine fired and Eagle rose from the Moon, like an elevator shooting up a tall building.

Meanwhile, Michael Collins circled the Moon in the command module, peering through his sextant and searching for the lunar module. Fortunately, it didn't take him long to spy Eagle. Soon, the two crafts began their space dance and carefully docked together. After moving moon rocks and soil into the command module, the astronauts released Eagle into space. The faithful lunar module that had taken Aldrin and Armstrong to the Moon was now dead weight that they couldn't afford to carry home.

A few hours later, Apollo 11 fired an

Command module and crew retrieved by USS Hornet

engine to move out of lunar orbit and start its journey home. On July 24, the command module reentered Earth's atmosphere in a blaze of fire, while Mission Control nervously waited to see if the heat shield had protected the crew.

One by one, three parachutes opened. As the command module splashed down in the Pacific Ocean, Mission Control broke out in celebration.

The men were retrieved by the Navy's USS *Hornet*, then immediately put in quarantine to protect the world from potentially dangerous "moon germs." But the astronauts were still warmly welcomed home by President Richard M. Nixon through a wall of protective glass. When the Apollo 11 crew was released from quarantine twenty-one days later, the

President Richard M. Nixon welcomes the Apollo 11 astronauts home. Left to right: Armstrong, Collins, Aldrin.

Celebration in Mission Control

country couldn't wait to see them. Throngs of people gathered to catch a glimpse of Aldrin, Armstrong, and Collins in huge parades held in New York, Chicago, and Los Angeles.

Across the country, and across the world, millions of others gathered around televisions to watch and join in the celebration. The moonwalking heroes were finally home!

Parade in New York City

Author's Note

This project would not have happened without the generosity and encouragement of many experts. I am greatly indebted to Apollo 7 astronaut Walter Cunningham, for answering questions about his incredible mission, and Apollo 12 astronaut Alan Bean, for sharing his time for two interviews about his Moon landing mission. My sincere thanks to Dr. David R. Williams, planetary scientist, NASA Space Science Data Coordinated Archive, Goddard Space Flight Center for reviewing the manuscript and directing me to an Apollo 1 recording to help determine the astronauts' last words, and to Luke Alexander, Aerospace Engineer, for vetting the text and sharing his expertise. With gratitude to Joel Kowsky, NASA photo editor and photographer, for his ongoing invaluable assistance. My appreciation to Brad Novak and Deborah Topolski for sharing their wealth of space knowledge, and a warm acknowledgment to my engineering coworkers/mentors at McDonnell Douglas Space Systems—Roy Lovejoy, Roger Papet, and Fred Grant. Thanks to NASA for making their Apollo mission transcripts and photos available. (Check out the *Apollo Flight Journal* and *Apollo Lunar Surface Journal* links in the Selected Bibliography for yourself!) I'm also deeply grateful to my editor, Kathy Landwehr, for her meticulous eye, really smart questions, and unending energy and passion.

Given the scope and unique design of this middle grade project, there were many details from my research about the missions, spacecraft, and Team Apollo that, after careful consideration, were not included. That's the ongoing conundrum of a nonfiction author, deciding which facts work best overall for a particular story and its intended readers, and which ones seem appropriate to leave out. I hope this book encourages readers to investigate and find out more about the remarkable Apollo missions and inspires people of all ages to pursue their dreams.

Illustrator's Note

While creating the illustrations in this book, I finally became aware, on an even deeper level than I had before, of the sacrifice, bravery, and dedication of the Apollo astronauts. I could only imagine what they saw and felt.

My goal was to depict moments from each mission as honestly as possible. With the help of an abundance of visual references, I set out to capture what the image would look like, balancing the need for accuracy with the need to display the power of the experience.

I could not be 100 percent sure that I had depicted every element correctly. In some cases, there were multiple accounts of the same event with slight variations. I listened to the astronauts' interviews and read their recollections to confirm details that varied from official records.

My goal is to create the illusion of being there. I typically start with a primitive rough sketch based on the text, then I collect all the available reference material. I carefully examine each image, concentrating on certain aspects of the setting, such as the light direction, contrast, and of course, any details that ensure accuracy. From there, I create the base in pastels, add watercolor, and finish with colored pencil. I use very fine-tip black markers to add or enhance final details and then airbrush any areas I feel need it.

In some cases, I felt that there was no way to truly capture the majesty of the flights, the power of the stage separations, the turbulence of the machines, and the dangers that the astronauts faced on every mission.

My deepest apologies to readers if a bolt is out of place, a piece of clothing is not exactly right, or the location of a crater on the Moon's surface is not quite accurate. I can assure you, however, that the emotional connection I felt to the persons involved in these amazing events is very real.

Selected Bibliography

Books

Aldrin, Buzz, and Malcolm McConnell. *Men from Earth*. New York: Bantam, 1989.

Cernan, Eugene, with Don Davis. *The Last Man on the Moon: Astronaut Eugene Cernan and America's Race in Space*. New York: St. Martin's, 1999.

Chaikin, Andrew. *A Man on the Moon: The Voyages of the Apollo Astronauts*. New York: Viking, 1994.

Holt, Nathalia. *Rise of the Rocket Girls: The Women Who Propelled Us, from Missiles to the Moon to Mars*. New York: Little Brown, 2016.

Kranz, Gene. *Failure Is Not an Option: Mission Control From Mercury to Apollo 13 and Beyond*. New York: Simon & Schuster, 2000.

Nelson, Craig. *Rocket Men: The Epic Story of the First Men on the Moon*. New York: Viking, 2009.

Reynolds, David West. *Apollo: The Epic Journey to the Moon 1963–1972*. New York: Harcourt, 2002.

Stafford, Thomas, with Michael Cassutt. *We Have Capture: Tom Stafford and the Space Race*. Washington DC: Smithsonian Books, 2004.

Websites

"Apollo 7 Air-To-Ground Voice Transcriptions," *www.jsc.nasa.gov/history/mission_trans/AS07_TEC.PDF*.

"Apollo Missions," *Lunar and Planetary Institute*. *www.lpi.usra.edu/lunar/missions/apollo*.

"The Apollo Program," *www.hq.nasa.gov/office/pao/History/apollo.html*.

E. Bell II, curator, *NASA Space Science Data Coordinated Archive*. Last updated October 5, 2016. *nssdc.gsfc.nasa.gov/about/charter.html*.

Anna Heiney, page editor, *Kennedy Space Center*. Last updated December 18, 2017. *www.nasa.gov/centers/kennedy/home/index.html*.

Eric M. Jones and Ken Glover, eds., *Apollo Lunar Surface Journal*. Last modified September 5, 2017. *www.hq.nasa.gov/office/pao/History/alsj/frame.html*.

"The Apollo Program," *Smithsonian National Air and Space Museum*. *airandspace.si.edu/explore-and-learn/topics/apollo/apollo-program/*.

David Woods, ed., *Apollo Flight Journal*. Last modified February 10, 2017. *www.history.nasa.gov/afj*.

Chapter 1: A Daring Dream

All quotations
"Excerpt from the 'Special Message to the Congress on Urgent National Needs,'" *www.nasa.gov/vision/space/features/jfk_speech_text.html.*

Chapter 2: The First Mission—Apollo 1

18 "Flame…bad fire"
"The Apollo 1 tragedy," *nssdc.gsfc.nasa.gov/planetary/lunar/apollo1info.html.*
23 "There's a…will work"
Francis French and Colin Burgess, *In the Shadow of the Moon: A Challenging Journey to Tranquility, 1965–1969* (Lincoln, Nebraska: University of Nebraska Press, 2010), 145.

Chapter 3: The Mission Continues

28 "If we…of life"
"NASA History, Detailed Biographies of Apollo I Crew - Gus Grissom," *www.history.nasa.gov/Apollo204/zorn/grissom.htm.*
31 "We would…the moon"
Gene Kranz, *Failure Is Not an Option: Mission Control From Mercury to Apollo 13 and Beyond* (New York: Simon & Schuster, 2000), 208.

Chapter 4: To the Sky—Apollo 4-6

32 "Five, four, have lift-off"
CBS News with Walter Cronkite *www.youtube.com/watch?v=1uoVfZpx5dY*
32 "The roar is terrific"
Douglas Brinkley, "The Voice of God on TV: Walter Cronkite's 1960s", *Newsweek* (March 19, 2012), *www.newsweek.com/voice-god-tv-walter-cronkites-1960s-63729.*
43 "The Apollo…men aboard"
"Urges Manned Earth Orbit of Moon Ship," *Chicago Tribune*, April 25, 1968.

Chapter 5: Risking it All—Apollo 7

All quotations
Apollo 7 Air-To-Ground Voice Transcriptions, *www.jsc.nasa.gov/history/mission_trans/AS07_TEC.PDF.*

Chapter 6: Aiming for the Moon—Apollo 8

All quotations

David Woods and Frank O'Brien, *The Apollo 8 Flight Journal*, *www.history.nasa.gov/afj/ap08fj/index.html*.

Chapter 7: Spider in Space—Apollo 9

86 "Alright, Houston…Good show"

David Woods and Andrew Vignaux, *The Apollo 9 Flight Journal*, *www.history.nasa.gov/afj/ap09fj/index.html*.

87 "Barfing anywhere…you die"

Craig Nelson, *Rocket Men: The Epic Story of the First Men on the Moon* (2009, New York: Viking), 211.

Chapter 8: Dress Rehearsal—Apollo 10

All quotations

David Woods, Robin Wheeler, and Ian Roberts, *The Apollo 10 Flight Journal*, *www.history.nasa.gov/afj/ap10fj/index.html*.

Chapter 9: Achieving the Dream—Apollo 11

Quotations on pages 106–126

David Woods, Ken MacTaggart and Frank O'Brien, *The Apollo 11 Flight Journal*, *www.history.nasa.gov/afj/ap11fj/index.html*.

Quotations on pages 127–133

Eric M. Jones *Apollo 11 Lunar Surface Journal, www.hq.nasa.gov/alsj/a11/a11j.html*.

Bringing Apollo 11 Home

138 "9, 8…6, 5"

Eric M. Jones *Apollo 11 Lunar Surface Journal, www.hq.nasa.gov/alsj/a11/a11j.html*.

Photo Credits

All photos are courtesy of NASA.

page 24
Grissom (s64-32110)
White (S64-31631)
Chaffee (S64-31447)

page 25
Top left: Grissom, Chaffee, White (S66-49181)
Bottom left: Technicians (s66-58023)
Bottom right: Command module (S67-21295)

page 44
Apollo 4 (6754387)
Apollo 5 (6762210)
Apollo 6 (S68-27365)

page 45
Top row: Saturn V (6757953), Apollo 4 (S67-50531)
Middle row: Mission Control (S68-18733), Apollo 5 (6862755)
Bottom row: view from space (as06-02-1436)
Command module (S68-26989)

page 56
Schirra (S62-05526)
Cunningham (S64-31816)
Eisele (S64-31469)

page 57
Top left: Saturn IB (s68-29781)
Apollo 7 crew (S68-42343)
Apollo 7 launch (S68-48662)

pages 72–73
Earthrise (as08-14-2383)

page 76
Borman (S64-31456)
Anders (S64-31555)
Lovell (S69-62241)

page 77
Top left: Saturn V (6761894)
Right: Borman, Lovell, Anders (6972185)
Welcome (S69-16402)

page 88
McDivitt (S71-59425)
Schweickart (S71-51265)
Scott (S71-52276)

page 89
Top left: Apollo 9 crew (KSC-68PC-302)
Top right: Mission Operations Control Room (S69-26301)
Bottom: Schweickart (as09-20-3094)

page 104
Stafford (s72-35016)
Cernan (s69-32614)
Young (s69-32616)

page 105
Top left: Apollo 10 (S69-27741)
Top right: Mission Operations Control Room (S69-34038)
Apollo 10 crew (S69-34329)

pages 112–113
Earth (as11-36-5355)

pages 130–131
Aldrin (as11-40-5875)

page 134
Armstrong (9018112)
Aldrin (S69-31743)
Collins (S69-31742)

page 135
Top left: command and service module (KSC-69P-247)
Right: Aldrin (as11-40-5903)
Bottom left: Armstrong (S69-38678)

page 136
Command/service module (S69-19190)

page 137
Space suit and PLSS backpack (S69-25878)

page 138
Hornet (S69-21294)

page 139
Left: Mission Control (s69-40023)
Top right: Armstrong, Collins, Aldrin, Nixon (S69-21365)
Bottom right: parade (S70-17433)

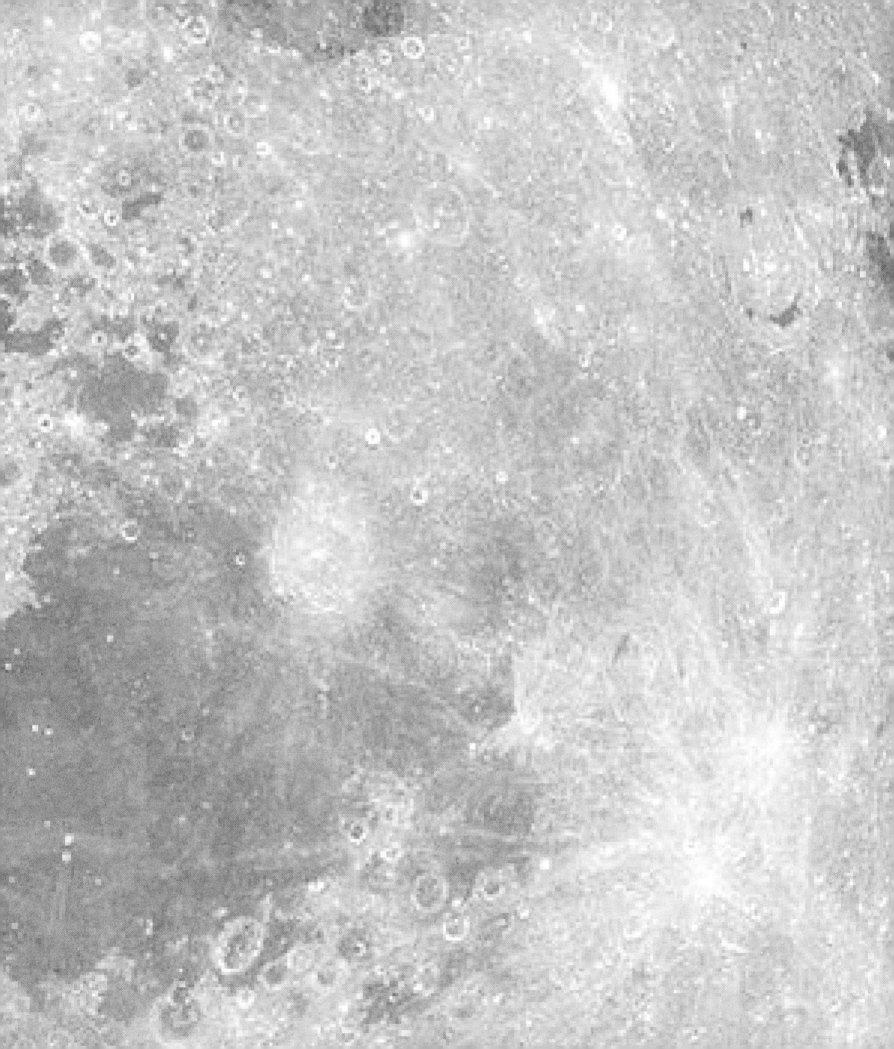

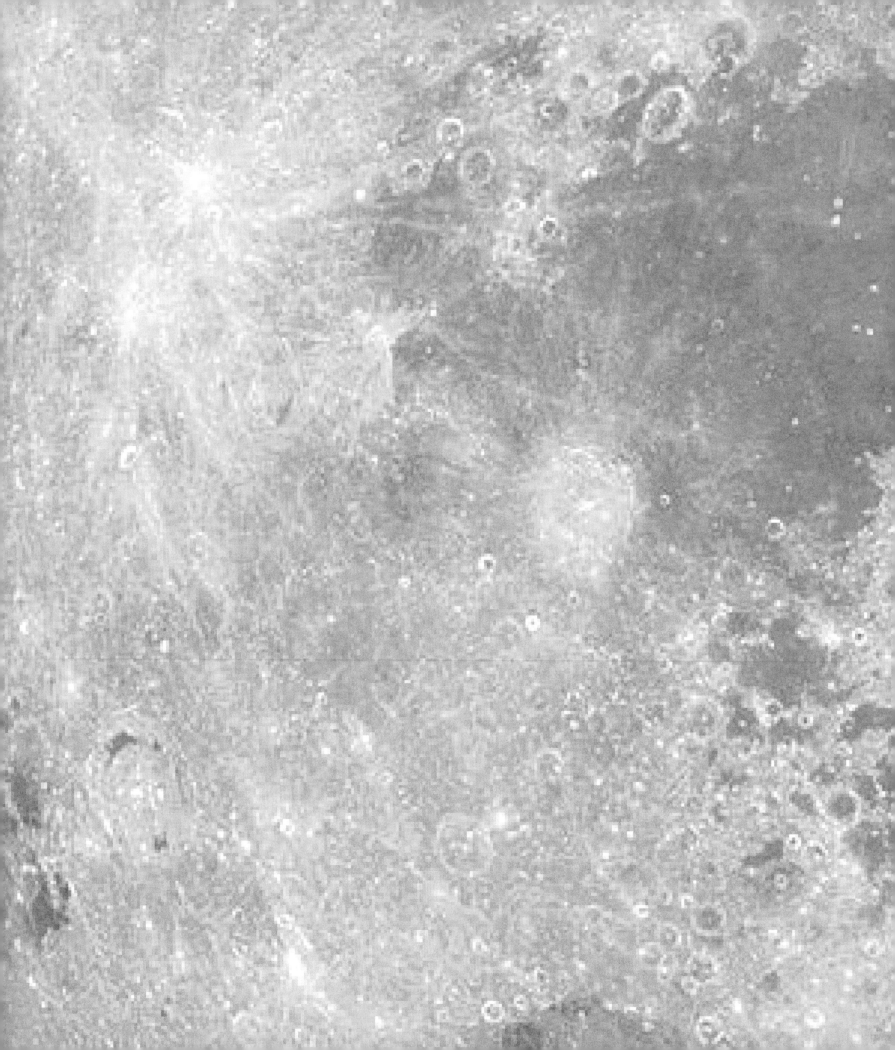